Soul of Lisbon

30 EXPERIENCES

AUTHORS: FANY PÉCHIODAT AND LAURIANE GEPNER

ILLUSTRATIONS: COLINE GIRARD

PHOTOS: PAULA FRANCO @LISBONBYLIGHT

JONGLEZ PUBLISHING

Travel guides

"FOR A LONG TIME,
WE KEPT THIS CODE WORD
TO OURSELVES: LISBON.

IF THINGS TOOK A BAD TURN,
THE WHITE CITY WOULD BE
OUR SAFE HAVEN."

OLIVIER FRÉBOURG

WHAT YOU WON'T FIND
IN THIS GUIDE

- the route of Tram 28
- the address of the Santa Justa elevator
- the most touristy dinner and fado show

WHAT YOU WILL FIND
IN THIS GUIDE

- the best vegetarian meal of your life
- a cocktail that will take you back in time
- the joy of running on clouds
- a party venue the size of a palace
- fifty shades of green in the middle of the city
- the low-down on cod
- the direct line to a bookshop from another world
- where to raise a glass with an old-timer

This guide is not comprehensive – and it doesn't aspire to be. There are other guides for that.

Our M.O. is the opposite of overwhelming you with options. Instead of suggesting 1,000 ideas you won't have time to explore in just a few days anyway, we've chosen just 30. Obviously, we were very tempted to stretch that to 40, or even 50 ... But we stuck to our guideline. As a result, we scoured Lisbon without counting our steps, climbed and hurtled back down hills, chatted with the characters who crossed our path, sampled every edible thing to be found in the city, drank a few nectars (guided by our professional code of ethics) and explored all the nooks and crannies, passages and alleyways ...

And here you are, holding the fruits of our labour in your hands. A selection of 30 experiences in Lisbon to savour, make your own and – we hope – love.

SYMBOLS USED IN
"SOUL OF LISBON"

< 10 euros

10 to 40 euros

> 40 euros

First come,
first served

Reservation
recommended

100% Lisbon

Opening times often vary,
so we recommend checking them directly
on the website of the place you plan to visit.

Some call it magnetic; others compare it to an aging woman who has lost almost all her finery but still has style. Some claim it's eternal; others that it's losing its soul as the face of the city changes. Maybe the truth can be found – as is so often the case – at the intersection of history, memories and dreams, both collective and personal. Somewhere in a tram lurching across the ages and hills; in the dusky pink of a façade in Mouraria, blushing as a ray of sunlight skims it just so; in the beating heart of the city, Chiado; in the cheeky humour of Graça; or in the majesty of Belém. In the *miradouros* perched on the city's highest points. And, finally, in the Tagus River, which flows into the ocean across which the great 15th- and 16th-century Portuguese explorers set sail and returned home.

Lisbon is like the movement of these waves, flowing between the open ocean and shore. Are we in a can't-miss capital of the start-up scene, a young and creative city, forward-looking and tech-driven? Or in one of Europe's oldest cities, covered with azulejo tiles, whose thousands of blue eyes have been watching us, unblinking, for several centuries? The answer is: both. Lisbon juggles with time, jumping from past to near future across two thresholds. Here, a supremely Instagrammable coffee shop with clean lines; there, a boutique that's been around since 1789 and still makes candles the old-fashioned way – today as it did yesterday, as it will tomorrow. Or maybe not: Lisbon's fate is cause for concern. The old boutiques are closing their doors; with each façade that is renovated, a bit more of the Lisbon of yesterday disappears.

Yet there's one thing about Lisbon that isn't ready to change: the light. So unique it could give anyone the crazy idea never to leave the city again – or to leave everything else for it. A light born of the reflection of the water on the Tagus, called the "Sea of Straw" (Mar da Palha) for its golden shimmer. A light that paints the cobblestones white, splashing across everything in its way, the façades dancing along with it like shadow puppets. Lisbon is written in this eternal light, of which one Lisbon native said, "I've never seen similar light anywhere else. Grey days are my favourite: the cobblestones are of such pure white they seem to be infinite in volume." She then went on: "Lisbon is a poem to look at." We'd add: "and to discover." And here are 30 experiences to prove it.

30 EXPERIENCES

BAIRRO ALTO

BAIXA CHIADO

Alfama

Ponte 5 DE ABRIL

Almada

#01

THE BEST-EVER
VEGETARIAN RESTAURANT

Created in 2019 by João Ricardo Alves, a Portuguese-Brazilian chef, and Alejandro Chávarro, a naturalised French Colombian, Arkhe is an exceptional experience. It's very likely the best vegetarian restaurant you've ever tried – and at perfectly acceptable prices, considering the quality of the food.

A great deal of thought, passion and incredible talent goes into everything at Arkhe. And you can look forward to a warm and impeccably professional welcome from Alejandro, who used to manage Michelin-starred restaurants in France and Spain and is also a top-class sommelier.

An absolute must.

ARKHE
RUA DE SÃO FILIPE NÉRI 14

+351 211 395 258

arkhe.pt

02

THE LISBON BISTRO
PAR EXCELLENCE

A little way from the touristy areas (which is a relief!), in the pleasant Campo de Ourique district, yet barely 15-minutes' walk from Principe Real, Bichomau is our kind of bistro: 100% Lisbon, with its pretty blue ceramic decor, excellent food (a new take on Portuguese cuisine) at reasonable prices and a charming atmosphere ... What more could you want?

One of our favourite places in Lisbon.

 BISTRÔ BICHOMAU
R. COELHO DA ROCHA 21A

+351 211 608 694   letsumai.com/widget/bistro-bicho-mau

#03

POCKET-SIZED BOOKSTORE:
3,000 BOOKS OVER 4 SQUARE METRES

In another life, Simão Carneiro was an oenologist. Since 2008, he has been spending his days in a former tobacco shop, which he has transformed into a tiny bookstore. Inside, you'll find more than 3,000 used books cheek to jowl, on sale for anywhere from 1€ to 1,000€ for the rarest editions. The space is so tiny that there's only room for one person at a time. What really matters can be found elsewhere – namely, between the pages of these books, which have been brought together with such passion by their owner.

NB: The undertaking itself isn't the only thing that's poetic; the opening hours are too. Give Simão a call before heading over to avoid finding the door locked.

LIVRARIA SIMÃO
ESCADINHAS DE SÃO CRISTÓVÃO 18

+351 961 031 304

Falta-me
um
sentido,
um
tacto

#04

A UNIQUE
TEA EMPORIUM

Located in a magnificent former 19th-century shoe shop, the Companhia Portugueza do Chá (Portuguese Tea Company) is a small gem: the moment you open the door, you're enveloped by the powerful scent of this leaf, which, according to the 5th- or 6th-century Chinese Buddhist monk Bodhidharma, promotes concentration and meditation.

Ensconced on lacquered shelves, the elegant tins hold 250 blends of tea: varieties from the most prized plantations in India, Nepal, Sri Lanka (Ceylon), China, Japan, Taiwan, Vietnam and Korea, as well as from Latin America, Africa and the Azores ...

The blends, flavoured with organic fruit or flowers, are created by the Argentinian owner, Sebastian Filgueiras. In his workshop at the back, Sebastian also regularly dreams up new flavours: Japanese yuzu and green tea, black tea with grapefruit, and fruit infusions that are perfect for enjoying iced.

€

 **COMPANHIA PORTUGUEZA DO CHÁ
R. DO POÇO DOS NEGROS 105**

+351 21 395 1614   companhiaportuguezadocha.com

- SEBASTIAN FILGUEIRAS -

FOUNDER OF COMPANHIA PORTUGUEZA DO CHÁ

Where did you get the idea for this tea emporium?

In Lisbon, small shops that combined the coffee and tea trades had become obsolete, and I wanted to revive this tradition by expanding the range of varieties available and constantly raising the quality. Catherine of Braganza (1638–1705), who made tea fashionable in Europe, has pride of place here: it's her profile that is featured on our tea tins. In the 18th century, every garden in the city had tea pavilions, a legacy of the strong ties between Portugal and the East.

What's your favourite tea?

The loose-leaf tea of my childhood – usually black tea from China, Assam or Ceylon. Strong teas. In northern Portugal, where my wife grew up, serving black tea to children before school – and in hospital too – was also very common. Very often it was tea from Mozambique or Ceylon. Tea bags didn't come along until much later.

What inspires your blends?

The light of this city, the culture of this country, its literature, its history ... I started with Lisbon Breakfast, a blend of Ceylon tea and black tea grown in the Azores. It's bright and well-balanced, a good everyday morning tea. Our Earl Grey Portugal is flavoured with the peel of bergamot grown on a farm in the Alentejo region: we dry it ourselves. Many of our teas are exclusive.

What's the rarest tea available here?

Thousand-Year Tea. It's grown in the Yunnan region of China, and what makes it unique is that its leaves are picked from a single tree, probably one of the oldest in the world. It's even listed as one of China's heritage tea trees. The taste is impossible to define – it's mild yet powerful. I put myself on a waiting list for this tea every year ... and never receive more than 2 kg.

# #
05

IF YOU'RE CRAZY
ABOUT COD

To understand the place of *bacalhau* (cod) in Portuguese cuisine, you have to start with this popular joke:

> 'There are a thousand ways to cook bacalhau.'
> 'No, there are 1,001! Don't forget, there's my recipe too!'

And cod has definitely found its place at this delicatessen, which dates back to the 19th century. On one side: cheese, wine and cold cuts. On the other: the best cod fished off the coast of Iceland, salted for varying periods of time (from 6 to 20 months). Sold by weight and sliced right in front of your eyes.

 MANTEIGARIA SILVA
RUA DOM ANTÃO DE ALMADA 1

+351 213 424 905   loja.manteigariasilva.pt

06

RUNNING LAPS
ON A ROOFTOP

Enter the hotel, walk confidently towards the elevator, get in and push the '-1' button. When you reach the spa, buy a day pass. Get changed and take the elevator to the 11th floor. A vision overlooking the Tagus: a running track on the roof. So you can race against the sun and challenge the clouds, legs in the air, eyes taking in a 360°-view of Lisbon. Pure magic.*

*Since this magic is on the pricey side, this 5-star running experience is a good gift idea. A day pass includes admission to the fitness room and spa. We guarantee that you (or the recipient of your gift) won't regret it.

© FOUR SEASONS HOTEL RITZ LISBON

€€€€

 FOUR SEASONS HOTEL RITZ LISBON
R. RODRIGO DA FONSECA 88

+351 21 381 1400   fourseasons.com

#07

EXPERIENCE
A SURREAL EVENING

About 15 minutes east of central Lisbon by taxi, in the Beato district, the Palacio do Grilo (Palace of the Cricket), which was classified as a monument of public interest in 2011, is a magnificent 18th-century palace. A few years ago, it was transformed into a spectacular restaurant-cum-nightclub with a deliberately surreal atmosphere.

During dinner, which is served in the palace's magnificent main rooms, expect improbable artistic performances amidst the tables. The food is decent – but that's not why you're here.

After dinner, at weekends, head for the nightclub, where the DJs and bar staff, donning costumes and sometimes masks, set the tone for a decidedly offbeat evening.

One-of-a-kind in Lisbon.

PALACIO DO GRILO

PALACIO DO GRILO – GALA CRICRI
CALÇADA DO DUQUE DE LAFÕES 1

+351 910 440 942   palaciogrilo.com   contact@palaciogrilo.com
                 galacricri.com   contact@galacricri.com

#08

THE BEST
BEACH CLUBS

When you think about Lisbon, beach clubs like those you typically see on Mediterranean islands don't immediately spring to mind. And yet: just a 20-minute taxi ride from central Lisbon, on the Costa da Caparica, from May to September you might almost think you're in Ibiza or on Mykonos.

Casa Reîa is Caparica's most successful beach club: excellent food, first-rate lounge music, perfect hippie-chic design and DJ nights at the weekend ... A far cry from fado and sardines.

A mere five-minute walk away, Princesa also serves quality food. And just five minutes further along the beach, Pôsto da Onda, with its pretty decor, is a lovely place for a drink.

To cool off between a couple of mojitos, we highly recommend going for a swim – the crystal-clear water is not as cold as you might think.

 CASA REIA – PRAIA DA CABANA DO PESCADOR COSTA DA CAPARICA

casareia.com – +351 937 346 841
We recommend reserving a table and a day bed in advance.
Surfboard rentals are available

 PRINCESA

praiaprincesa.com

 PÔSTO DA ONDA

postodaonda.com

#09

UNCOVER THE SECRET
SPOT WHERE FADO SINGERS HIDE AWAY

First, you find yourself facing a heavy blue wooden door adorned with a gilded handle: magisterial, intimidating. Then you attempt to open it before realising that you have to ring the bell. Someone opens the door for you. It's here, in the dim interior of this 18th-century building decorated with old azulejo tiles, that the city's fado singers meet up after having sung their hearts out elsewhere.

The musicians gradually trickle into their sanctuary. Around 11pm, a fadista sings the saudade accompanied by two guitar players, linking gesture with voice, emotion with the expression in their eyes ... A few minutes later, another voice, other musicians, will take over, but the thrill remains the same: fado. And the performance doesn't let up until sleep finally wins out – sometimes at 2am, sometimes not until breakfast.

MESA DE FRADES
R. DOS REMÉDIOS 139

+351 917 029 436

mesadefrades.pt

MESA DE FRADES

# #
1º

THE TEMPLE OF
PORTUGUESE
NOUVELLE CUISINE

Prado means 'meadow' in Portuguese. And that's where chef Antonio Galapito, aka the rising star of Portugal's food scene, takes his inspiration. After having learned the ropes with chef Nuno Mendes in London, Galapito now champions 'cuisine libre' (free cuisine) at his Lisbon restaurant, inspired by the farm-to-table movement. Ingredients that come from all across the country, dishes whose composition changes daily depending on the season and the chef's mood ... The only constant: the flavour of Portugal today.

© RODRIGO CARDOSO

- ANTONIO GALAPITO -

CHEF AT PRADO

What's your oldest cooking-related memory?

I was born near Sintra, where suckling pig is a specialty. Maybe even more than the taste, it's the smell of it that makes my mouth water ... My mother would grill it over a wood fire, and you could smell the aroma of garlic, paprika, white wine, and black pepper.

Do you serve it at Prado?

Sometimes, but cooking it for seven to eight hours in a normal oven is a bit more technical. The way we serve it is also different from the traditional recipe: meat, sauce, and ... that's it. Bye-bye, trimmings. The meat is so tender, there's no need for anything else.

When did you know you wanted to become a chef?

When I was 14, I was terrible at school. I wasn't passionate about cooking; I didn't even particularly love eating – in fact, for me, a good steak was a well-done steak, which gives you some idea ... But that's when my mother suggested I go to cooking school. So I went – and never looked back.

And if you were to do something else ...?

No, I don't see myself doing anything else. Or maybe a farmer, when I'm 60 years old?

Is Prado a Portuguese restaurant?

Yes, to the extent that we source all of our ingredients (except for sugar) from Portuguese food producers all across the country. That's our only rule, and we build our menu – which changes a bit every day, depending on what gets delivered and our inclinations – around it. When we see new fish, we always ask if it was caught in Portuguese waters. If not, we don't take it!

Your à-la-carte guilty pleasure?

It varies every day, but some dishes are always on the menu and don't change much. One of my favorites (maybe even my absolute favorite!) is the bread, served with a paste made of goat's-milk butter, smoked coarse salt, pork fat, garlic, and caramelised onion compote ... I can't get enough of it!

A fun fact about Portuguese cuisine?

The Portuguese have always been great travelers. Did you know that they brought tempura to Japan? And when they returned from their expeditions, they brought back yuzu, which now grows in Portugal. We use it in the Prado kitchens instead of lemon: it immediately transports you to another place.

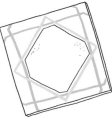

#11

BRING HOME SOME
AZULEJO TILES

After noticing so many azulejo tiles everywhere, you may find yourself wanting to see them ... in your own home. Make a beeline for this boutique, a family business that takes tiles very seriously. From 1979 to 2013, Joaquim José Cortiço's company sold large series of azulejo tiles. Then, in 2016, four of his grandchildren relaunched the business.

In their store, you can find old series produced in factories that have since shut down. Some of them are on the verge of disappearing, with just a few tiles left. By buying them, you engage in responsible consumption: the boutique doubles as an association that is committed to preserving and distributing its collection of azulejos.

CORTIÇO & NETOS
RUA MARIA ANDRADE 37D

+351 21 136 2376　　　　corticoenetos.com

RESTAURANTE PONTO FINAL

PONTO FINAL
CAIS DO GINJAL 72
CACILHAS
ALMADA

+351 21 276 0743

#12

GRILLED FISH
AT PONTO FINAL

A short boat ride and 15 minutes later you're in Cacilhas, on the other side of the Tagus. Grab the table at the very end of the pier, directly across from Lisbon. Murmuring water, the light of the final hours of the day, the simplicity of grilled fish with just a twist of lemon … If this isn't happiness, it sure comes close.

A VIDA PORTUGUESA
LARGO DO INTENDENTE PINA MANIQUE 23

+351 213 473 060

avidaportuguesa.com

#13

LISBON'S BEST
CONCEPT STORE

This is the Portuguese answer to Eataly – but not just for edibles. This concept store, the biggest of the four spaces created on the initiative of Catarina Portas, brings together the best artisanal products from all over Portugal. Its 500 square metres progress through an evolution from one room to the next. First, there's the living room, where the wool blankets will make you want to settle down for a nap; then you take a turn towards the kitchen, between ceramics and gourmet food products, before finally ogling the stationery items and ointments. Everything has been carefully selected and is beautifully presented. We double dare you to leave empty-handed.

© CHIADO

#14

SPEND A NIGHT AT
SANTA CLARA 1728

There are places that exist beyond the limits of time, trends and words. The Santa Clara 1728 hotel is one of them. Within the walls of this 18th-century palace, six rooms and a table d'hôte straight out of a minima-list dream are a blend of white, beige, blond wood and authentic period stone. Outside, in the world at large, our attention is constantly being solicited. Here, behind the Santa Clara's large doors and its windows overlooking the National Pantheon, in these rooms in which nothing is superfluous, silence reigns, the mind grows calm and sets sail, the soul takes flight ... Which is one definition of luxury.

© NELSON GARRIDO

SANTA CLARA 1728
CAMPO DE SANTA CLARA 128, RC

+351 932 251 056

silentliving.pt/houses/santa-clara-1728

SANTA CLARA 1728
© PIERRE VERDOUX

HOTEL MONTECARMO 12

The pretty rooms, each equipped with an elegant, understated stone bathtub, are arranged around the beautiful spiral staircase that encapsulates the soul of this revamped historic residence in the heart of the Principe Real district.

They serve a delicious breakfast too.

 HOTEL MONTECARMO 12
TV. MONTE DO CARMO 12

The reception is closed after 5 pm on weekdays; guests can access the hotel with a code and a beep

montecarmo12.com

- JOÃO RODRIGUES -

MANAGER OF THE SILENT LIVING GUESTHOUSES

João Rodrigues juggles gracefully. In addition to his career as an airline pilot, he also owns four exceptional guesthouses in Portugal, including Santa Clara 1728 in Lisbon. We met him over a classic breakfast.

What made you want to open guesthouses?

When I was little, my parents' home was always open and filled with people. That inspired me for the future!

What's the story behind Santa Clara 1728?

The first time I saw this building, it was under renovation. I climbed the façade and that's when I fell for the view: the National Pantheon on one side, the convent and monastery of São Vicente de Fora on the other, and, in the far background, the Tagus. I knew I had to live here and open a guesthouse in this old neighborhood tucked between Alfama and Graça.

How would you define the 'Silent Living' philosophy?

It permeates Santa Clara, whose large volumes recall

© PHILIPPA LANGELY

an ancient monastery. It's about respecting traditional architecture and materials, developing a minimalist esthetic around them, and distilling an atmosphere that's reminiscent of a family home ... And, at the heart of this philosophy is the idea that when you enter here, you leave behind the hustle and bustle and demands of the outside world – everything that disturbs peace of mind.

What's your view of Lisbon?

The Tagus embraces the city, opening its arms wide to it. That's what moves me most about this city: its connection to the water. And for me, as someone who is always on the move as part of my profession, Lisbon is the home that welcomes me with open arms every time I return.

Your favorite places?

The Gulbenkian Museum, its gardens, which are the work of Portugal's best landscape designers. I also love Belém, even though it has changed over the years. When I try to go back to a place, I'd like to reconnect with my memories; often it isn't possible because it has closed down or been replaced ...

Is that what's meant by *saudade*?

Yes. It has to do with our history, the age of great discoveries in the 15th and 16th centuries. People left, and you never knew if they would return. That's the origin of this feeling of absence, this nostalgia – a powerful emotion.

One last Lisbon secret?

The best time to enjoy the city is ... in February. The streets are emptier, time is distilled more slowly, and the light is as gorgeous as ever.

\#15

ONCE A PALACE,
NOW A PARTY

Imagine a large, slowly crumbling building where it's party time every day (almost) – and on every floor. On the first floor, the DJ is having as much fun as the people who've come here to dance to the pop, soul and disco music he's spinning ... And from the bar to the terrace, with its large rooms divided into small alcoves for private heart-to-hearts, the building, funded by an association, is an oasis for free and curious spirits.

Check out the programme (concerts, DJ sets, projections) and get there before 11pm so you don't end up watching the party ... through the windows.

One last bit of advice: growing real-estate pressure means that Casa Independente's days may be numbered. So run, don't walk – before it's too late.

© MARTA PINA

CASA INDEPENDENTE
LARGO DO INTENDENTE PINA MANIQUE

casaindependente.com/nos
info@casaindependente.com

Instagram: @casa_independente

#16

SINK YOUR TEETH
INTO A *BIFANA*

A *bifana* is to the Portuguese what a ham-and-cheese sandwich is to the British: a simple, quick and inexpensive solution that rarely disappoints. It consists of a very finely sliced pork cutlet, marinated in dry white wine, lemon juice, bay leaves, paprika and garlic, and gently basted in its own juices, nestling between two slices of *papo seco* (Portuguese bread). To spice things up, spread on some mustard right before you sink your teeth into it and then wash it down with a few glasses of wine. For an even more decadent experience, bite into a *leitão*, a typical Portuguese sandwich made with suckling pig.

For *bifanas*:
**AS BIFANAS DO AFONSO
R. DA MADALENA 146
LISBOA**

facebook.com/pages/
Bifanas Do Sr. Afonso/650766081654855

For *leitãos*:
**NOVA POMBALINA
RUA DO COMERCIO, 2
LISBOA**

+351 21 887 4360

NOVA POMBALINA

- FELIPA ALMEIDA AND ANA ANAHORY -

FOUNDERS OF THE INTERIOR DESIGN STUDIO ANAHORY ALMEIDA

How do you see the artisanal crafts in Portugal today?

They are the subject of renewed interest today, both from local young people and foreigners who arrive and view them with enthusiasm, without preconceptions. All the better, because most of the artisans of the older generation that we've met in the context of our projects tell us that few young people want to learn what they have to pass on. But that's changing.

How do you begin an assignment?

For our projects, we use almost exclusively furniture and materials from Portugal. As a result, every assignment begins with a search for artisans. What's funny is that most of those we try to contact don't have an e-mail address. To meet with them, we sometimes have to head off to the middle of nowhere, to the other side of the country.

How do you combine Portuguese tradition with today's codes??

We ask traditional artisans to add a twist to their creations by revamping patterns and integrating original colors into them. It's a process that's not without its risks and surprises, but that's exactly how we like it!

What's your view of Lisbon's creative scene?

It's coming back to life, from new art galleries to contemporary ceramics studios ... And we're very happy about it since it means more people for us to collaborate with.

Is Lisbon a source of inspiration?

Every day. We walk around the city a lot, slipping into the entrance halls of buildings and old boutiques to understand how the materials were used at the time. And we always take pictures of old ladies at old bars! We don't find our inspiration on Instagram – which is also what we try to explain to our clients ...

One absolute must-see?

The up-and-coming Marvila neighborhood, a haven for galleries, young artists' studios, and artisans' workshops. And, in a completely different vein, the Palácio dos Marqueses da Fronteira, which we discovered recently: a 17th-century hunting palace covered with magnificent azulejo tiles.

BAIRRO DO AVILLEZ

17

SOAK UP
THE ATMOSPHERE
OF PRAÇA DAS FLORES

Just a five-minute walk from the hectic and touristy Praça do Principe Real, Praça das Flores is one of Lisbon's loveliest squares.

There are three ways to soak up its atmosphere: sit quietly on one of the benches in the centre of the square, surrounded by trees; savour a delicious orange juice and *pastel de nata* from the square's kiosk (for local residents who might not know, opening an account at the kiosk entitles you to a substantial discount on all your purchases ...); or enjoy a very pleasant lunch at the café-restaurant Magnolia in the north-west corner of the square, ideally sitting on the small terrace or at the charming table for two by the large window that opens onto the square.

 MAGNOLIA BISTROT & WINEBAR
PRAÇA DAS FLORES 43

+351 935 315 373
Instagram: magnolia_lisboa

 QUIOSQUE LISBOA
PRAÇA DAS FLORES

quiosquelisboa.pt/flores

MESTIÇO (MIXED-RACE) CAFETERIA

Fasten your seatbelts, we're off to one of Portugal's former colonies: Mozambique. In her little restaurant, chef Jeny Sulemange treats diners to food that feels like a hug. More specifically: beef samosas (we could eat them by the dozen), whole-grilled-shrimp samosas seasoned with lemon and coriander, chicken nestling in peanut sauce and coconut with delicately fragrant rice ... everything pure sunshine. Guaranteed to make you say *'Kanimbambo'* (Thank you) on your way past the kitchen.

CANTINHO DO AZIZ
R. DE SÃO LOURENÇO 5

+351 21 887 6472   cantinhodoaziz.com

#19

DO YOU DARE TO EAT
A SPIDER CRAB?

A little heads up if you want to try spider crab prepared Lisbon style: get ready to abandon all dignity. The spindly creature is presented to you before it is cooked. When the finished crab arrives, the show begins. Armed with a hammer, you break the shell to excavate the meat, dip it into a delicious sauce made of mayonnaise, mustard, egg, parsley, soft bread, pickles and a pinch of chilli pepper, and then spread the whole thing onto a slice of toast slathered with butter. A culinary delight that's not without its risks: you might very well end up with a bit of crab in your hair or on your shirt. Don't say we didn't warn you. If patience isn't your forte, choose one of these other *marisqueiras* (seafood restaurants), which take reservations : Nune's Real Marisqueira or O Relento.

CERVEJARIA RAMIRO **AVENIDA ALMIRANTE REIS 1 – H**	**NUNE'S REAL MARISQUEIRA** **R. BARTOLOMEU DIAS 112**	**O RELENTO** **AV. COMBATENTES DA GRANDE GUERRA 10C** **OEIRAS**
+351 969 839 472 cervejariaramiro.com	+351 21 301 9899 nunesmarisqueira.pt	+351 21 411 4063

#20

SEE A FILM
UNDER THE OPEN SKIES

Around when the sun sets over the Tagus, one of the great pleasures Lisbon has to offer is watching a film in an open-air cinema.

> CINE SOCIETY
Perched on the rooftop of the Cine Society, with the city as a backdrop, settle back comfortably into a deckchair with a cocktail in hand as you prepare to (re)discover a classic film under the stars.

> LA CINEMATECA
The Cinemateca has the best film programme in Portugal, hands down. And, in summer, it also screens quality films on a delightfully secluded terrace, taking you on a real trip back in time, far from the tourist crowds. Before the screening, you can also dine alfresco and visit the Cinemateca bookshop, a paradise for film buffs.

Open-air films generally start at around 9:30pm. As a general rule, you must purchase tickets on site and cannot reserve them in advance – with one exception: if you book a table for dinner on the terrace just before an evening screening, you can also reserve tickets for the film.

CINE SOCIETY
TOPO CHIADO
TERRAÇOS DO CARMO

Reservations recommended
cinesociety.pt

CINEMATECA
RUA BARATA SALGUEIRO 39

Programme: cinemateca.pt/Programacao.aspx
Tickets can be reserved by booking a table for dinner: contact the restaurant 39 Degraus
+351 960 396 370 or + 351 911 904 075

#21

LET THE NIGHT FLY BY
AT DAMAS

Although its name translates as 'ladies' (and also 'draughts'), Damas is no place for squares and it has quickly joined the ranks of the city's most trendy bars. Behind the pink neon sign over the door, Damas comes alive in two rooms, two atmospheres. The first is a bar-cum-restaurant with Middle Eastern influences which dispatches good food and inspired cocktails. To move on to the second one, follow the hallway shrouded in darkness that leads to the back room. Here, minimal music concerts, underground sounds and DJ sets fire up the hip 'The 90s are back' crowd. The perfect place for telling yourself that the night is still young.

DAMAS
R. DA VOZ DO OPERÁRIO 60

+351 964 964 416

damas.lisboa@gmail.com
Instragram: @damas.lisboa

#22

GO FOR A STROLL
IN THE ESTUFA FRIA

The greenhouse in the north of Eduardo VII Park is reminiscent of a Rousseau painting. Huge plants tickle the sky. Well, almost – this is a greenhouse, after all, so wooden blinds form a roof overhead ... even as they let the sunlight filter in. Come late in the afternoon, when the day is gently fading and the sky turning pink. To the left of the central alley, a small door leads to the arid and tropical greenhouse (Estufa Fria). Giant banana plants, cactuses that defy all norms ... Where in the world are we? Right in the heart of the city!

© ROXANE DE ALMEIDA @LAROXSTYLE

ESTUFA FRIA
PARQUE EDUARDO VII

+351 21 817 0996

#23

HAVE A DRINK IN
AN ABANDONED FACTORY

Nestled in the heart of an abandoned factory in the centre of the Alcantara district, Mīrārī is a multipurpose destination that is still relatively unknown.

From Thursday to Monday, this large open-air space at the end of a cul-de-sac hosts concerts, pop-up markets, boules competitions, exhibitions and a range of street-food options (pizza, burgers, poke bowls, artisanal ice creams, etc). On the back wall, a beautiful mural by Franco-Congolese artist Kouka Ntadi Assis completes the decor.

 MĪRĀRĪ
AVENIDA 24 DE JULHO 170

+351 960 260 890

mirari.pt
hey@mirari.pt

VAGO
© LUIS GALA

LISA
© @SHOTBYTEJA

#24

MUSIC, COCKTAILS
AND TAPAS

Opened in late 2021 by globetrotting DJs of Colombian, Brazilian, Turkish and Portuguese heritage, Vago is just what Lisbon's nightlife scene was missing. In the early evening, head here to listen to a fantastic music programme (house, techno, samba, zouk, afrobeat …), have a drink (great cocktails) and eat delicious *petiscos* (Portuguese-style tapas) created by chef Leonor Godinho. Later in the night, come to dance – and more.

Run by the same owners, Lisa is just a few buildings further down on the same street. Every night, it features live DJs and musicians playing jazz, contemporary music, rock, folk, electro and more.

VAGO
RUA DAS GAIVOTAS 11

+351 916 500 060
Instagram: @vago.lisboa

LISA
RUA DAS GAIVOTAS 5

salalisa.pt
Instagram: @a.sala.lisa

THREE BAR STOOLS,
ONE BAR

It's a Portuguese spirit(s)ual question, but there is a world beyond port wine. And, in this world, Ginja, or Ginjinha (sour-cherry liqueur), holds centre stage. For a long time, the Ginjinha Sem Rival (Unrivalled Ginjinha) bar, which opened in 1890, made its own in the back shop. And the question customers are asked the moment they rest their elbows on the counter hasn't changed since the 19th century: 'Com o sem elas?' (With or without cherries?) We recommend with – even though (or especially because) it's dangerous! Your little glass will be served filled to the brim, as tradition dictates. As for whether or not it's truly the best Ginjinha, you'll simply have to head across the street to try out the neighbouring bar's version for yourself ...

GINJINHA SEM RIVAL
R. PORTAS DE SANTO ANTÃO 7

+351 21 817 0996

#26

ROOMS WITH VIEWS:
LISBON AT YOUR FEET

Put your heart-to-heart with Lisbon on hold for the night? No, thanks. Instead, choose to fall asleep with Lisbon at the foot of your bed and wake up to the same vision, daytime version. Here is a selection of rooms we recommend:

MEMMO ALFAMA

This hotel is hidden away in the Alfama district, at the end of a cul-de-sac paved with uneven cobblestones. Up on the roof terrace, slide into the red swimming pool to do a few laps with a view. And in rooms 31 and 33, the Alfama is right there at the foot of the bed, a labyrinth of rooftops unfurling all the way down to the Mar da Palha (Sea of Straw).

© MEMMO ALFAMA

MEMMO ALFAMA
TV. MERCEEIRAS 27

€€€

150–360€/night   +351 21 049 5660   memmohotels.com/alfama

TOREL PALACE

A great location at the top of the Hill of Sant'Ana, just a few steps from the Jardim do Torel. Regardless of what room you're staying in, the terrace, swimming pool and royal peace and quiet await you. But we recommend putting your bags down in room 6, 8 or 28: big windows, small balcony and an insane view of the heart of the city.

© TOREL PALACE

TOREL PALACE
R. CÂMARA PESTANA 23

110-350€/night | +351 21 829 0810 | torelpalacelisbon.com

MEMMO ALFAMA

 # 27

SMALL CAFE,
WIDE ANGLE

Exploring, walking, climbing, running ... That's all well and good, but where's the R&R in all this? It's right here, at this cafe under a theatre. Take a little break and settle down in one of the armchairs facing the enormous windows – just long enough to bring your heart rate back down, check in with yourself and drink a latte while taking in the panoramic view of Lisbon.

**CAFÉ DA GARAGEM
TEATRO TABORDA
COSTA DO CASTELO 75**

+351 21 885 4190

Instagram: @cafe.dagaragem
teatrodagaragem.com/en/cafe-da-garagem

CAFÉ DA GARAGEM

PASTÉIS DE NATA VS ELEPHANT EARS: **SHOWDOWN OF THE SWEETS**

PASTÉIS DE NATA

If Lisbon had a flavour, it would be the *pastel de nata* (custard tart) – never mind that this pastry was actually invented in the 19th century by nuns in the convent in Belém (which was still separate from Lisbon at the time). Since 1837, the Pastelaria de Belém has been carrying on this tradition, selling these *pastel de Belém* pastries to the hordes of tourists who come here to taste the original – the one that started it all. But you can also avoid a long wait: at the Aloma pastry shop and tea salon, which has won the prize for best *pastel de nata* more than once, the custard tarts are prepared on the spot, served lukewarm, dusted with cinnamon ... and polished off at the counter in less time than it took to write this sentence. For the most patient among you, treat yourself to the pastel de nata at the superb Jardim da Estrela, located close by.

📍 **PASTELARIA ALOMA**
R. FRANCISCO METRASS 67

📍 **PASTELARIA O CARECA**
R. DUARTE PACHECO PEREIRA 11D

Instagram: @pastelaria_aloma
aloma.pt

+351 21 301 0987
pastelariaocareca.pt

ELEPHANT EARS

Above Belém, in the Restelo neighbourhood, the Pastelaria O Careca is a local institution. Regulars throng to what they call 'the Bald Guy' – the nickname given to the man who originally opened the place in 1954. The price of success? You now have to take a number at the door and wait a few minutes for your turn – just long enough to peruse the amazing display case before choosing the house speciality: elephant-ear cookies. But not just any old elephant ears, the best in town: the perfect balance of flaky, toasted, lightly caramelized, crunchy and sweet.

#29

TALK TO STRANGERS
AT PROCÓPIO

Since 1972, the little red door to this nightclub has seen many insiders pass through, here to lose all sense of time. In fact, in the small room, where waiters flit about in bow ties, styles and centuries seem to collapse in on themselves: tasselled lampshades brush against armchairs, knick-knacks flirt with illustrations from the 1930s ... To make sure you don't miss a thing, choose the table at the back perched on a small platform or a seat at the bar, while sipping a Caipï or Amendoa Amarga.

NB: Since we're still sort of stuck in 1972 here, smoking is permitted.

 PROCÓPIO
ALTO DE SÃO FRANCISCO 21

+351 21 385 2851

barprocopio.com/pt

#30

JUST LIKE HOME (PORTUGUESE STYLE)

Welcome to Zé da Mouraria, which for 20 years has been treating diners to its little world. In a room covered with family photos (in the broadest sense of the term: the restaurant's regulars), a solo lunch guest is told, "For you, half a portion. It's a lot, but we can't make any less."

Bacalao asado (roasted cod) accompanied by chickpeas, potatoes and onion chips, all of it generously doused in olive oil, appears on the chequered tablecloth. Enough to feed ... well, yes, a family. But the best part is still seeing clusters of Portuguese of all generations and backgrounds passing each other dishes across the long tables in a fabulous familial hubbub.

To be a part of it, make sure to get there at noon on the dot. Even then, you might have to wait outside on the street, a glass of chilled white wine in your hand ...

📍 **ZÉ DA MOURARIA**
R. JOÃO DO OUTEIRO 24

+351 21 886 5436

MUITO OBRIGADO / MANY THANKS TO

Jérôme C, João-Maria MS, Sofia M, Peter O, Chloé S, Miguel C, Miguel J, Alexander W, Nelson P, Rita A, Luca P, Ruben O and Anne-Laure B

This book was created by:
Fany Péchiodat and Lauriane Gepner, authors
Nathalie Chebou, project manager
Coline Girard, illustrator
Paula Franco @lisbonbylight, photographer
Stéphanie Benoit and Emmanuelle Willard Toulemonde, layout
Jason Briscoe – Unsplash, cover photo
Clémence Mathé and Roberto Sassi, publishing
Sophie Schlondorff, translation
Jana Gough, editing
Kimberly Bess, proofreading

You can write us at contact@soul-of-cities.com
Find us on Instagram @soul_of_guides

In the same collection:

Soul of Amsterdam

Soul of Athens

Soul of Barcelona

Soul of Berlin

Soul of Kyoto

Soul of Los Angeles

Soul of Marrakesh

Soul of New York

Soul of Rome

Soul of Tokyo

Soul of Venice

© JONGLEZ 2024

Registration of copyright: March 2024 - Edition : 02

ISBN: 978-2-36195-651-6

Printed in Slovakia by Polygraf